☐ **W9-CYV-708**

Copyright © 2007 Scholastic Inc.

an imprint of

■ SCHOLASTIC

www.scholastic.com

Scholastic and Tangerine Press and associated logos are trademarks of Scholastic Inc.

Published by Tangerine Press, an imprint of Scholastic Inc., 557 Broadway; New York, NY 10012.

Scholastic Canada
Markham, Ontario

Scholastic Australia
Gosford, NSW

Scholastic New Zealand
Greenmount, Auckland

Scholastic UK
Coventry, Warwickshire

10 9 8 7 6 5 4 3 2

ISBN-10: 0-439-93467-2
ISBN-13: 978-0-439-93467-1
Printed and bound in China

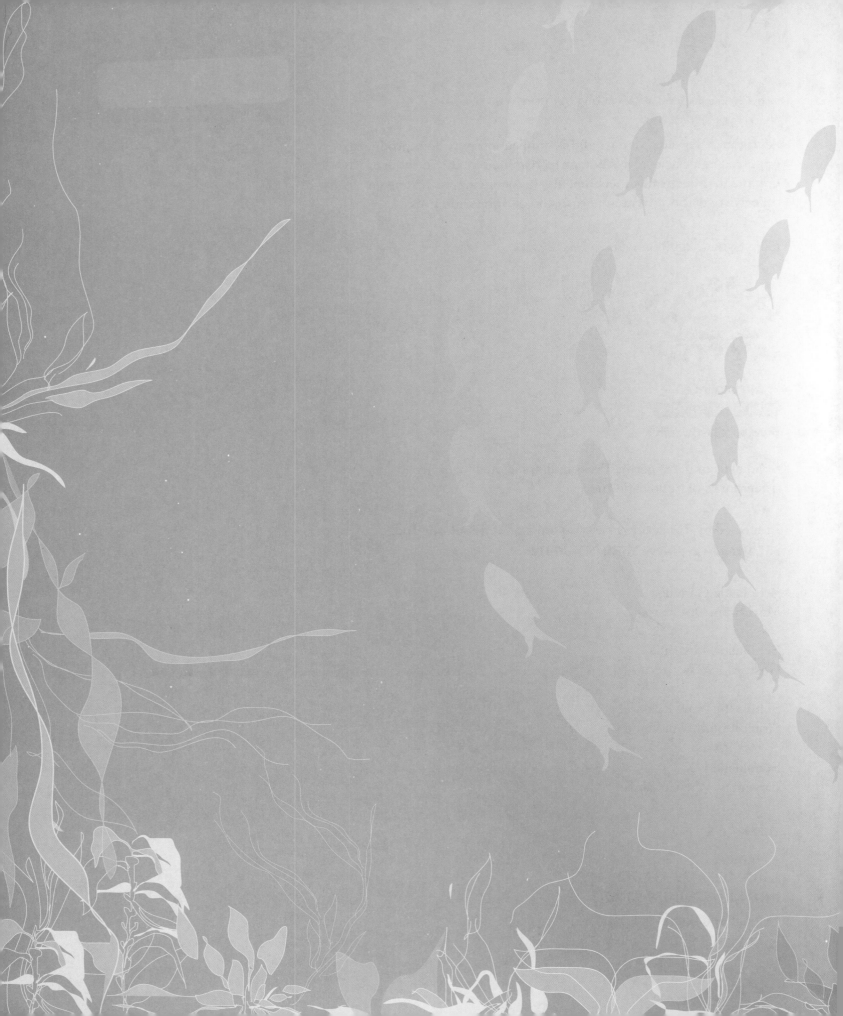

CONTENTS

How To Draw Sharks And Their Prey

"Shark" is probably the one word that evokes the greatest fear in people. Did you know that sharks have existed for over 350 million years? That's over 100 million years before the dinosaurs did!

Sharks are found in every ocean of the world and can also be seen in some rivers and lakes. There are about 368 species, and each species has its own unique shape, size, color, habitat, personality, and other attributes.

Almost all sharks are carnivores, which means that they eat meat. Bottom-dwelling sharks eat sea urchins, clams, and crabs that live on the ocean floor. Open-water sharks hunt squid, fish, other sharks, sea birds, and marine animals.

In this book, you'll learn how to draw a few of these amazing creatures and also some of their prey. Drawing requires a lot of patience and practice, so stick to it! You'll get better and better with each try. So, grab some paper and sharpen your pencils—you're about to draw some of the most incredible animals in the ocean!

MATERIALS

One of the nice things about drawing is that you need just a few basic supplies, like the ones in your kit. Before you begin, be sure you have all your materials handy so that you don't have to stop work for, say, an eraser.

1. PAPER

Grab a stack of blank white sheets of paper in the size of your choice. Choose paper that isn't glossy or textured. Professional drawing paper works great if you don't mind the expense.

2. PENCILS

You can pick up a set of good quality drawing pencils, including HB, 2B, 4B, and 6B. An HB pencil comes with this kit. The lighter HB and 2B pencils work best for basic drawing and for the finishing touches. The softer pencils, like the 4B and 6B, are used to add shading. Create a number of shades with just one pencil (like the HB) by decreasing or increasing the pressure.

3. ERASER

Keep a white eraser with sharp edges handy. Use the eraser not only to fix mistakes, but also to add highlights and textures.

4. SHARPENER

Any type will do. You always want to have sharp points on your pencils for the cleanest drawings.

DRAWING TECHNIQUES

One of the most important things when it comes to drawing is to be comfortable with your materials.

1. First, try out the different pencils. Study the different strokes, line thicknesses, and how dark you can draw with your pencils.

2. Choose a soft pencil like a 2B, 4B, or 6B and try drawing straight parallel lines—vertical, diagonal, reverse, and horizontal. Practice this across a couple of pages, letting your hand move freely. This exercise may look too easy, but don't skip it because it will help you get comfortable with the drawing pencils.

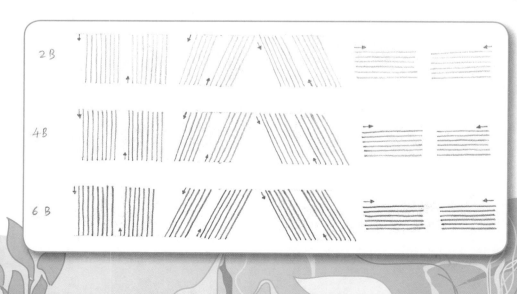

3. Practice drawing ovals and circles of various sizes. Use a 6B for this exercise. Draw the shape in one stroke, and draw it quickly. Use both sides of the paper and continue practicing for a while before starting to draw. Using quick, single strokes gives you a good judgment of form and volume, and makes your drawing more confident.

Note

You can use ordinary paper for these exercises. Don't use an eraser!

SHADING AND HIGHLIGHTING

1. Before you start shading, decide on the source of light. Shade the portions on the opposite side of the light, keeping in mind the volume of the drawing. If the shade portion is not rendered according to the surface or bulge of the animal, the drawing will look flat.

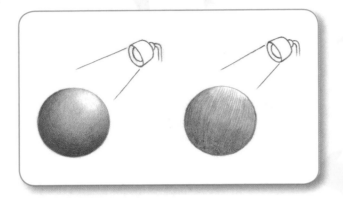

2. Shade doesn't necessarily mean black. It simply means less light. Try this exercise with all grades of pencils. Start shading horizontally or vertically, first using light pressure and then a heavier force. This will help you see the various tones you can achieve with the different pencils, which allows you to control your pencil according to the requirement.

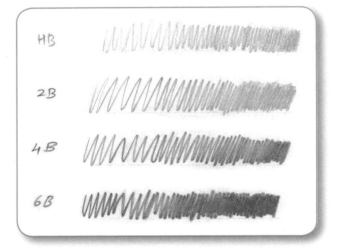

3. You can add dark lines for the deepest folds or ground shadows once all the shading is done. This will enhance your drawing and make it look more three-dimensional.

4. A highlight is the brightest part of an object, where there is maximum light. It should be drawn in the direction of the light source. The highlighted area is to be left white, while the rest of the image is shaded. Highlights, especially of the eyes, add life to the image. If you forget to leave the highlight, just use the edge of your eraser to erase in the highlight!

TEXTURES

Every surface has a texture—smooth, scaly, rough, or hard. Animals have textures, too (furry, scaly, feathery, or hairy). Practice shading by holding a pencil in different positions. Try this with all of your pencils to get an idea of the variety of textures that can be achieved by simply changing the direction and grip of the pencil.

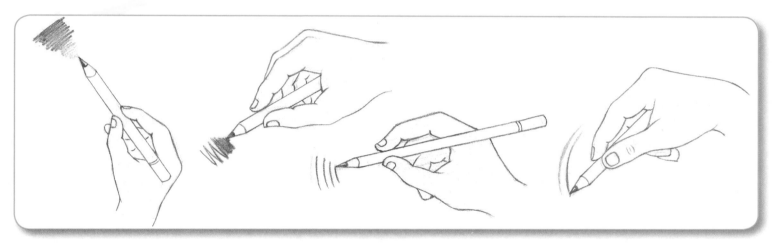

GILLS: The gills follow the shape of the body in a slight curve. Shade along these lines with gradations from light to dark tones. Add an extra dark tone (4B pencil) along the line and gradually fade out toward the end.

EYE: Shade the entire eye with a 4B or 6B pencil and leave a little dot for the highlight.

TEETH: Teeth are white, so you only need to add shade according to the source of light. Use an HB pencil for the shaded area, which won't be very dark.

FINS: Use a 2B or 4B pencil for rendering smooth textures. Make sure you avoid making bold or rough strokes. You can darken the fin toward its slightly uneven outlines.

GREAT WHITE SHARK

The great white shark (*Carcharodon carcharias*) is found along temperate coastlines around the world. It has a torpedo-shaped body, pointed snout, crescent-shaped tail, five gill slits, an anal fin, three main fins, and 3,000 teeth! Reaching lengths of about 20 feet (6 m) and weighing almost 4,000 pounds (2,000 kg), the great white is the world's largest predatory fish. It eats many different animals, including fish, seals, sea turtles, and rays.

Step 1

To draw this particular angle of the shark, start with an elongated conical shape. Note the slight bulge given to the triangular form. Spend some time to get this volume right as your entire artwork depends on these preliminary lines.

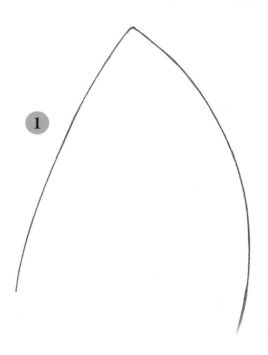

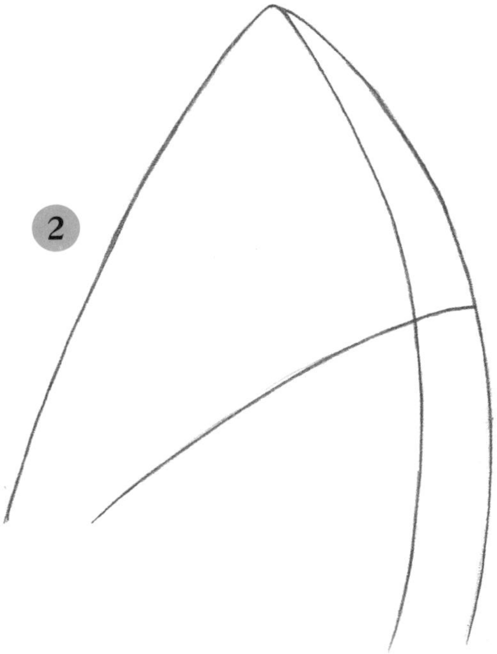

Step 2

Draw two lines along and across the conical shape. The vertical line should be more toward the right side and the horizontal should run up from a lower point of the head. Add slight curves to these lines to give the cone a rounded dimension.

Step 3

Mark the mouth area by roughly drawing a semi-oval that takes up most of the area. Just concentrate on the broadly divided forms and the relative proportions.

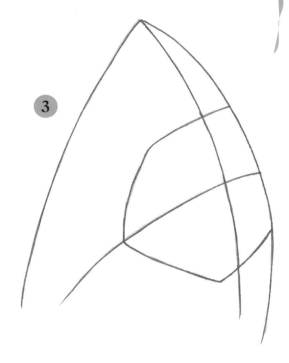

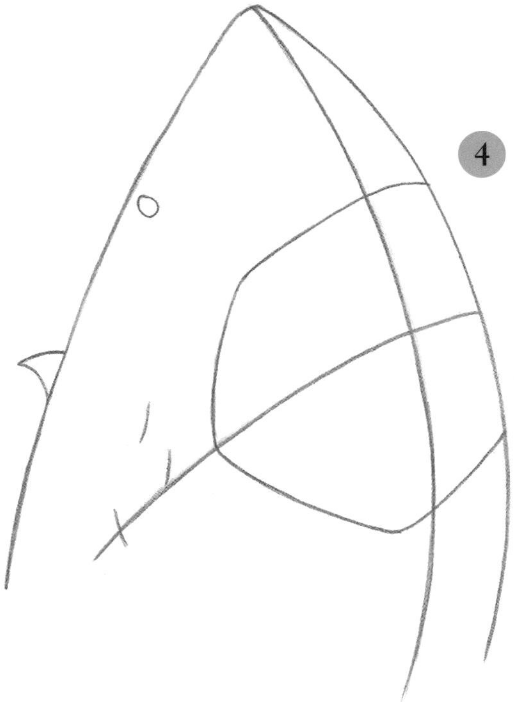

Step 4

Notice the perspective of the head and position the eye toward the outer, upper end of the cone. Draw the tip of the dorsal fin a little below the eye.

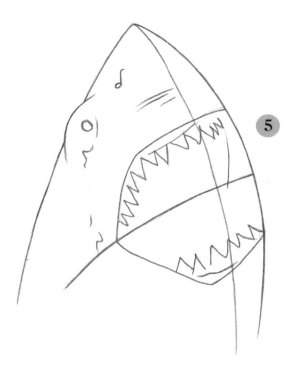

5

Step 5

Lightly add details like the teeth, the blowhole, and the skin texture. Remember that the great white shark's teeth point inward.

Step 6

Once the basic sketch is in place, erase the unwanted lines and detail the contours, the eye, and the jaws. Make sure you have all the details in place before starting to shade.

6

Step 7

Now start shading your drawing. The inside of the mouth is the darkest. The teeth need to be shaded individually, leaving a highlight on one side depending on the source of light. Also, notice the color difference on the back of the head.

7

Details

• Teeth

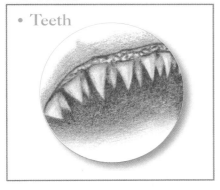

The teeth of the great white shark are its most striking feature. The most important thing is to get their volume and angle right. The individual teeth are shaped like inverted triangles, isolated from each other. Remember to keep your sense of perspective—teeth that are closer are slightly larger than the ones that are farther away.

• Eye

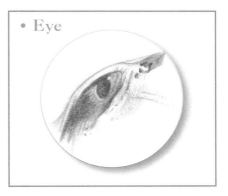

The eye of the great white shark is a small, dark, oval structure, not very prominent or protruding. Notice the slightly lighter curve along the eye, showing the thickness of the skin.

SEAL

The harbor seal is related to walruses and sea lions and has short, thick fur. It's found along shorelines in the North Atlantic and Pacific Oceans in temperate, subarctic, and arctic waters. It grows to be up to 6½ feet (2 m) long and can weigh up to 375 pounds (170 kg). The seal's whiskers help with its sense of touch. This animal is prey for great white sharks.

Step 1

Start by drawing a circle with a square below it. Note the size of and distance between the two. Draw these shapes lightly with a soft pencil as these will be references for your drawing.

Step 2

Add a smaller circle inside the first one, resting toward the lower right area.

Also add a dimension in perspective to the square as shown.

Step 3

Join the outer circle and the square with simple curved lines. Also curve off the extended square to form the body of the seal as shown. Draw all lines and shapes keeping in mind that your drawing is three-dimensional. This will help you with the volume and shape of the animal.

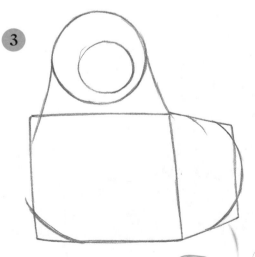

Step 4

Add two tiny circles for the eyes along the smaller circle drawn earlier. Draw a curving line down the middle of the small and big circle. Draw a small, upside-down triangle along this line for the nose. Also draw the mouth, using the center line as a guide. Add the flippers to the lower portion of the body.

Step 5

Fine-tune the drawing by adding details such as folds around the mouth, back, flippers, whiskers, and pores around the nose.

Step 6

The seal has shiny dark skin, so the shading has to be very smooth. There should be more dark to middle tones with a couple of strong highlights on the head. The overall effect should be that of a fat, rounded, shiny body.

SEA TURTLE

Sea turtles live in shallow coastal waters of warm and temperate seas. They are cold-blooded animals and have four flippers and a shell attached to the backbone. Sea turtles can be 2 to 6 feet (0.5 to 1.9 m) long and usually weigh between 78 to 1,900 pounds (35 to 870 kg). These reptiles are food for great white sharks.

Step 1

Draw a slightly curved horizontal line to give an idea of the size of the sea turtle you are going to draw. You can use a soft pencil that will help you get a smooth stroke.

1

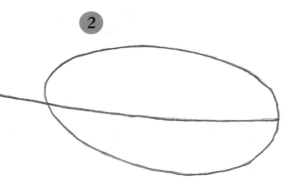

Step 2

Now draw an oval across more than ¾ of this line for the shell. Leave the rest of the line for the head. You can use the same soft pencil to draw these basic guidelines. Draw these lines lightly.

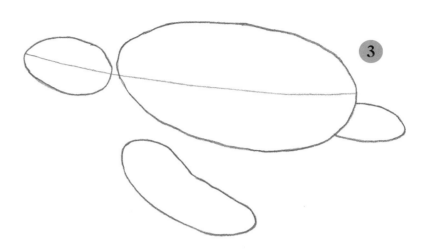

Step 3

Draw a small oval along the rest of the horizontal line for the head. Add one more oval at the rear for the tail and a longer one for the turtle's front flipper. Pay attention to the relative position and proportion of these shapes to the main body.

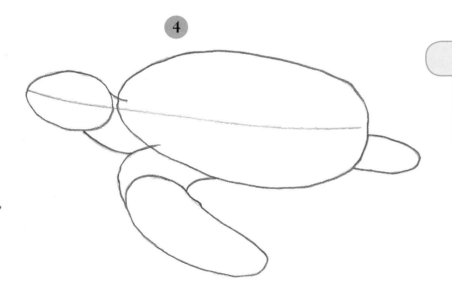

Step 4

Now join the ovals to the body. Be sure to draw these "joints" in sync with the basic structure drawn earlier. Take note of the overlapping lines, as these will be your reference lines for shading. (For example, the joint line of the front flipper comes over the line of the neck.)

Step 5

Now add a tiny circle for the eye and a slit for the mouth. Define the contours of the flipper, tail, head, and shell along the basic drawing. Also erase the guidelines as you gradually move toward a more detailed drawing.

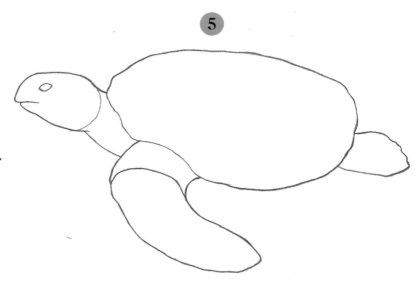

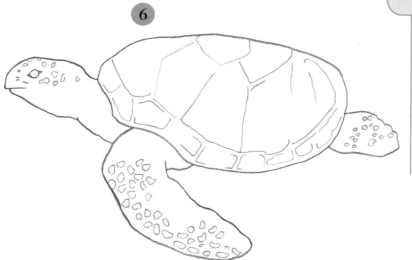

Step 6

Using a very light pencil, draw rough ovals to form the pattern on the shell. Note that these shapes are larger toward the top of the shell and smaller toward the bottom. Also detail the spotted texture on the head, flipper, and tail.

Step 7

You can now start shading the image. The surface of the shell is hard, so use rough pencil strokes. The texture of the skin area is smoother, so use gentler strokes.

Details

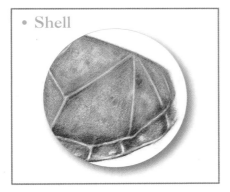

- Shell

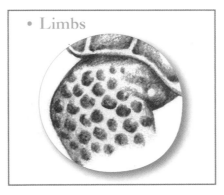

- Limbs

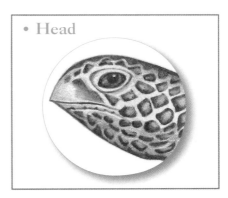

- Head

The surface of the sea turtle's shell is hard. Use a 4B pencil with rough strokes to get the effect. The patterns on the shell are larger toward the top and smaller toward the lower portion.

The limbs are covered with spotted skin that emerge from below the shell; note the overlapping lines. Sketch the dark patches with gentle strokes using a 4B pencil. Render the shaded area using a 2B or 4B pencil in mid-tones along one side of the limb. Shadows add even more depth.

The head is oval and slightly pointed at the mouth. It's covered with dark patches. The eye is dark and round with a darker pupil. Remember to darken the ends of the eye to give it depth.

SHORTFIN MAKO

The shortfin mako shark (*Isurus oxyrinchus*) has a bluish back and a white underside. This shark is usually 9 to 13 feet (2.75 to 4 m) long and can weigh up to 1,750 pounds (800 kg). The shortfin mako is known for its speed and ability to leap out of the water as it hunts its prey, which includes swordfish, tuna, other sharks, and squid.

Step 1

Start by drawing a line with a gradual upward curve for the line of reference. This line will determine the position and perspective of the shark.

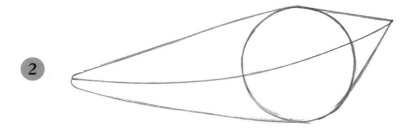

Step 2

Draw a medium-sized circle around the area where the arc slopes upward, leaving half an inch of the line jutting out on the right side. Note that the circle should be roughly divided into two halves by the line. Draw two tangents to the circle joining at the tips of the line segment to the right and the left. You now have a double conical shape that will be your basic structure for the shortfin mako.

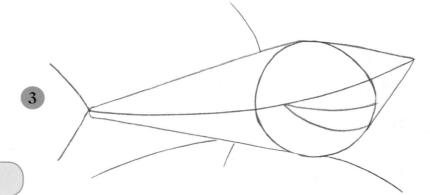

Step 3

Lightly draw an open jaw inside the lower half of the circle. The curve of the lines suggest the three-dimensional shape. Mark the lines for the fins, keeping in mind the overall direction and proportion.

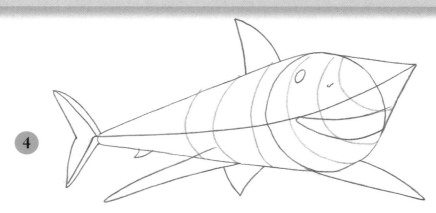

Step 4

Draw parallel arcs within the conical shapes to give a feel of the volume of the body. Mark the eye and nostril in the upper half of the circle. The eye of the shortfin mako is a little larger than that of some other sharks. Draw the fins at this stage.

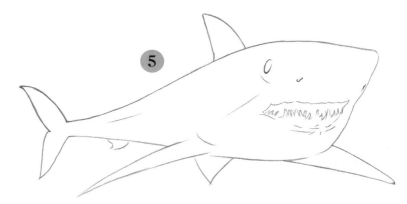

Step 5

Using the guidelines, draw the final shape and details of the shark and erase all reference lines. Add teeth to the lower jaw and define the shape of the mouth. The overall effect should be that of a fat, rounded body.

Step 6

You can now start shading the image from light to dark tones. The darkest tones will be inside the mouth and nostrils. Note that the upper half of the mako is darker and the lower is white. Use a 2B or 4B pencil and work on the smooth, shiny texture by rendering softly.

HAMMERHEAD SHARK

The great hammerhead shark (*Sphyrna mokarran*) is found in tropical and subtropical waters worldwide. It has a wide, thick, rectangular "hammer" head with eyes at the ends. This shark's eyes are about three feet (.9 m) apart! The average great hammerhead shark can grow up to 11½ feet (3.5 m) long and weighs over 500 pounds (230 kg). This fearsome hunter feasts on fish, rays, squid, octopus, crabs, lobsters, and other sharks.

How To Draw Sharks And Their Prey

1

Step 1

Start with a single line as reference for the pose and direction of the shark. Your entire drawing will be based upon this line.

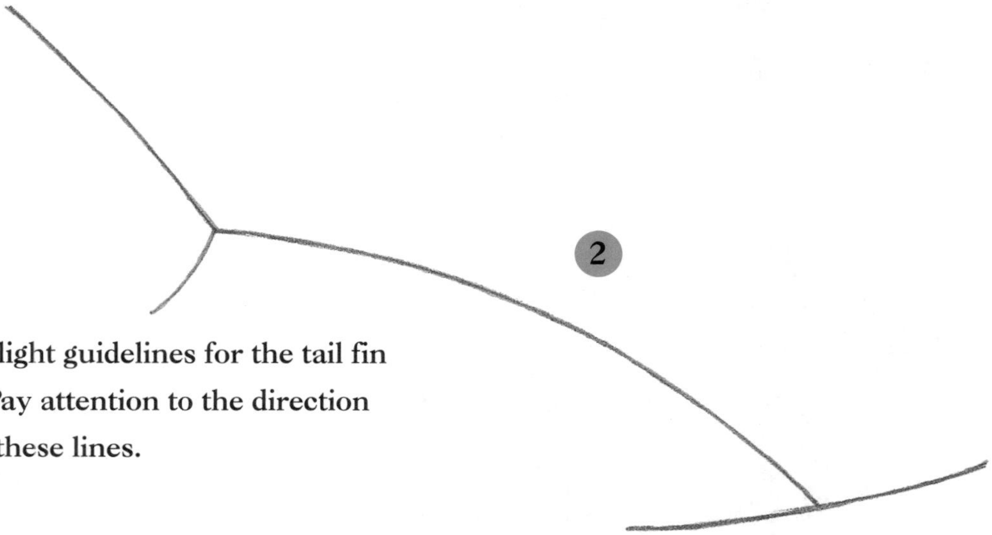

2

Step 2

Draw very light guidelines for the tail fin and head. Pay attention to the direction and size of these lines.

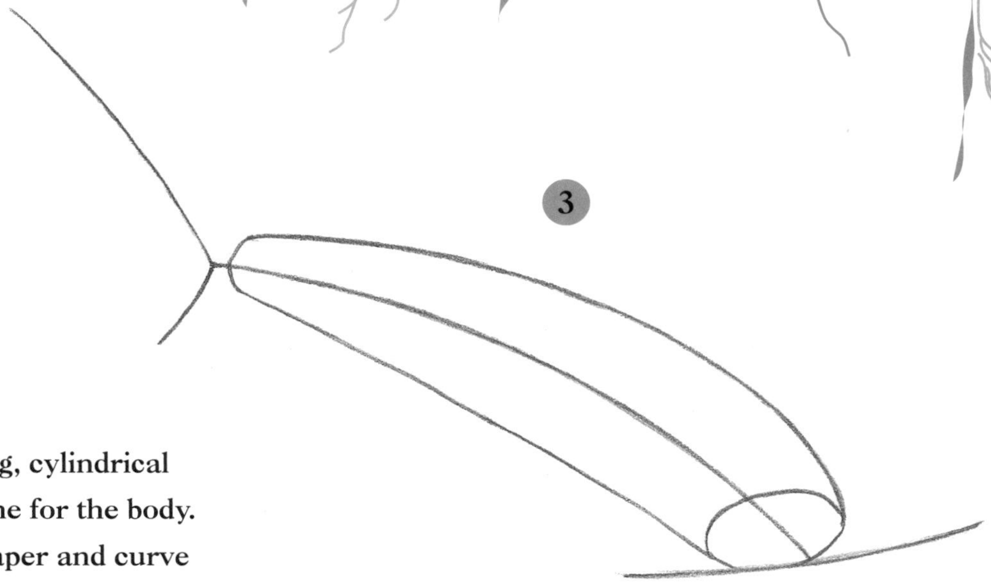

③

Step 3

Now draw a long, tapering, cylindrical shape along the central line for the body. Let the shape gradually taper and curve toward the end.

Step 4

Draw a rectangular box for the head and two triangles—one big and one small with their bases merged—for the tail fin. You've been drawing the basic shapes to get the volume and proportion of the shark right, so don't worry about the details yet!

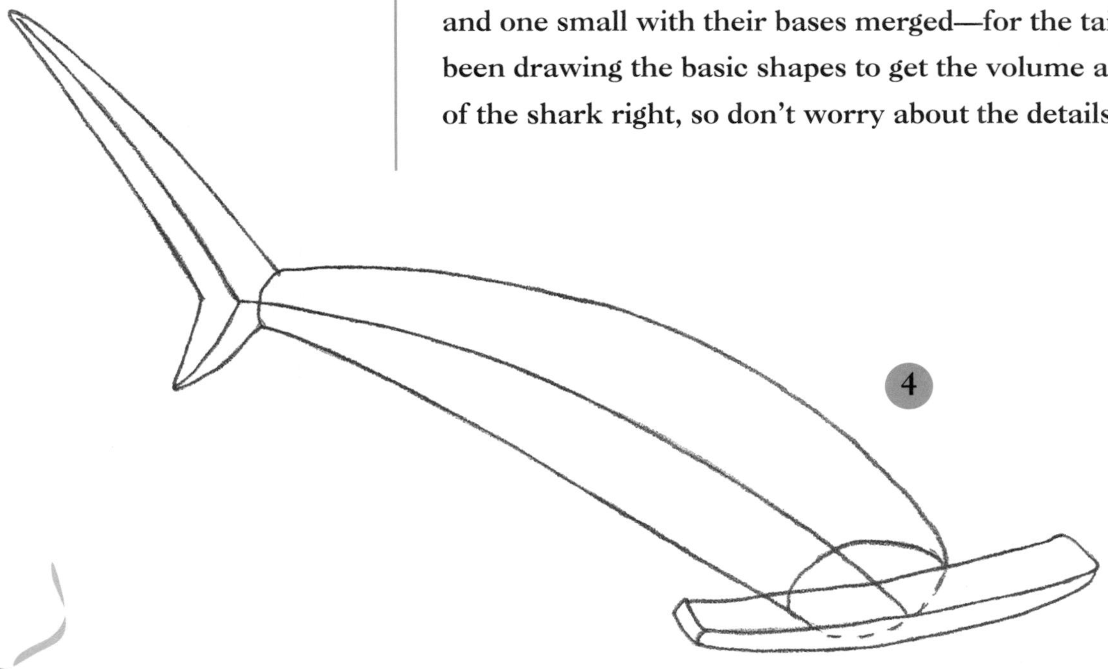

④

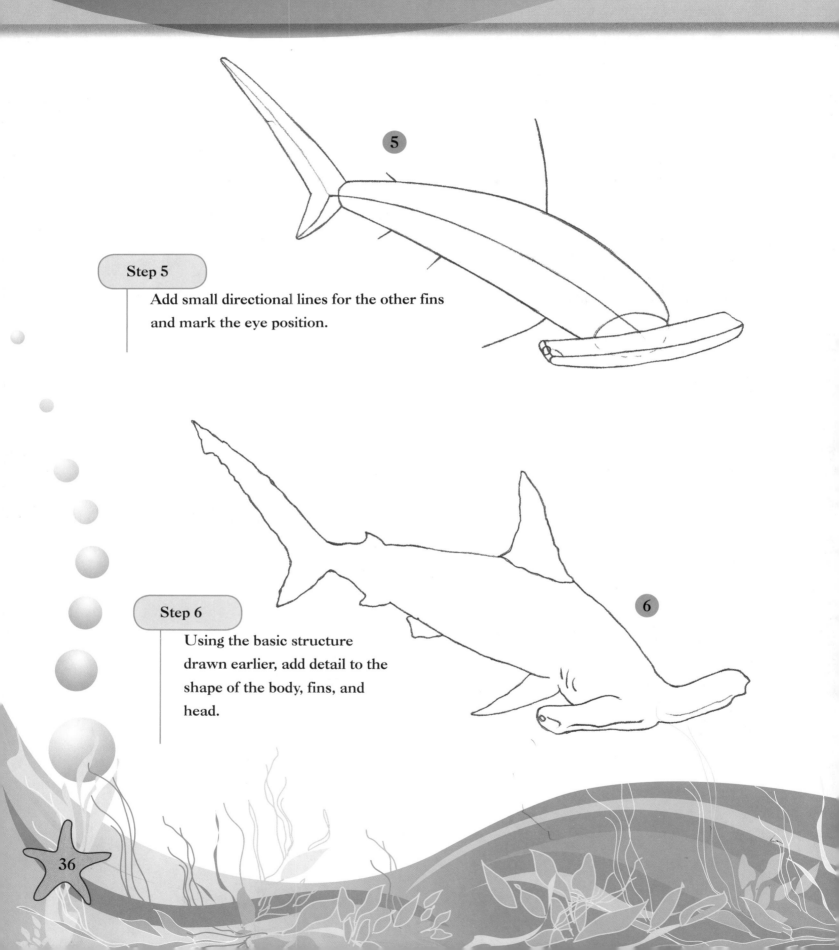

Step 5

Add small directional lines for the other fins and mark the eye position.

Step 6

Using the basic structure drawn earlier, add detail to the shape of the body, fins, and head.

Step 7

Now begin shading. First decide on the light source so you know where to add the highlights and shadows. Add the dark tones gradually, keeping in mind the three-dimensional volume of the shark. Try to feel the underlying volume of the shark so your drawing doesn't look flat.

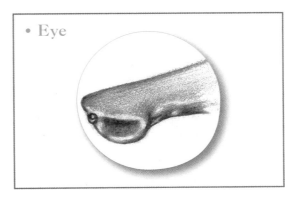

Details

• Tail

The hammerhead shark's tail fin is made up of two triangles with merged bases. It's slightly thicker where it joins the body. Maximum light will fall on this area. The smaller, lower fin appears midway on the shark's body and has a smooth texture.

• Eye

The hammerhead's eyes are located at the tips of its head. Shade around the circle and toward the top of the inside of the circle. Leave the rest of the inside white for the highlight.

OCTOPUS

The octopus is an eight-armed animal. It has blue blood, an eye on each side of its head, and if it loses an arm, it can regrow another! The biggest is the giant octopus, which can grow to be 23 feet (7 m) and weigh up to 400 pounds (182 kg). The smallest is the Californian octopus, which is only $^3/_8$ inch (1 cm) long. Octopuses are prey for the hammerhead shark.

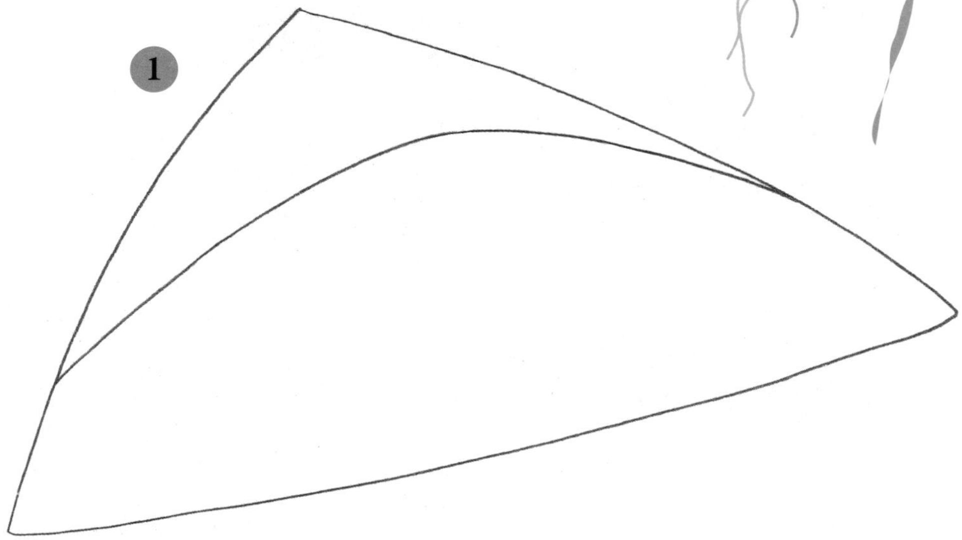

Step 1

Start by drawing a triangle with a slight bulge. This will be approximately the size of the octopus. Add an arc across the triangle to divide it into two parts.

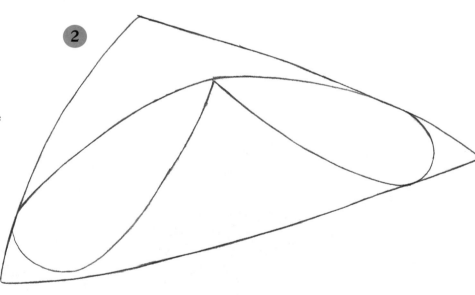

Step 2

Starting from the base of the arc, draw a curvy "W" like the one shown in the figure.

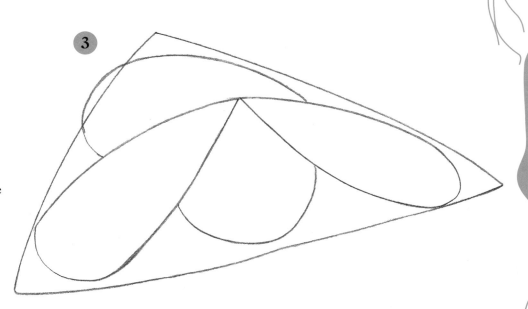

Step 3

Now add two more arcs to this image. One arc will sit on top of the central arc, and the other will be in the space created by the "W" you drew in Step 2. This is the basic form for the octopus.

Step 4

Start adding details to this outline, such as the curls of the tentacles and placement of the eyes. These aren't the final lines, so draw them using light pencil strokes.

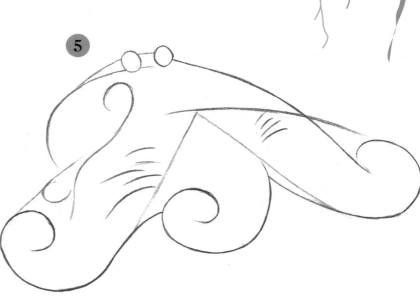

Step 5

Make your drawing more specific by adding exact volume to and defining the pose of the tentacles. Also add the folds of the skin. Erase the triangle you drew to get the basic sketch of the octopus.

Step 6

You can now add details to your drawing. Draw suction cups on the undersides of the limbs. Add some spots on the skin of the octopus.

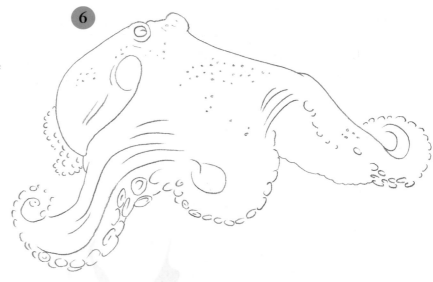

7

Step 7

Now you're ready to start shading. Notice the darker area on the lower side of the octopus. Gradually add dark tones on the upper portion of the octopus's body, keeping a single source of light in mind. Draw the eyes of the octopus on top of the head, paying special attention to the elongated pupil.

Details

• Limbs	• Skin	• Eye
	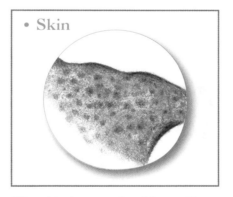	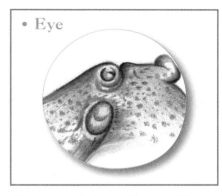

The octopus's limbs are fleshy and emerge from a single point and curve toward the end. Shade them like curved pipes, alternating shadow and highlight.

The skin is smooth with small dark spots. Decide on a single light source and shade opposite the light. Make sure the contrast of light and dark is more prominent in the skin folds. Finally, tap your pencil on the shaded area to create the dark spots.

The eyes stick out like marbles in thick skin. Draw a small circle surrounded by concentric circles to show the skin folds. Shade the eyelid with darker lines along the skin folds. Also leave a white ringed highlight on the skin around the eyeball.

STINGRAY

Rays have a flat body, long tail, and no bones! The smallest ray is the short-nose electric ray, which is about 4 inches (10 cm) wide and weighs around 1 pound (0.5 kg). The biggest is the manta ray, growing to over 22 feet (6.7 m) wide and weighing several tons. There are about 70 known species of rays, and many are food for great white and hammerhead sharks.

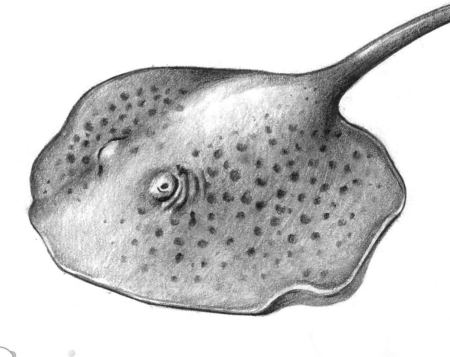

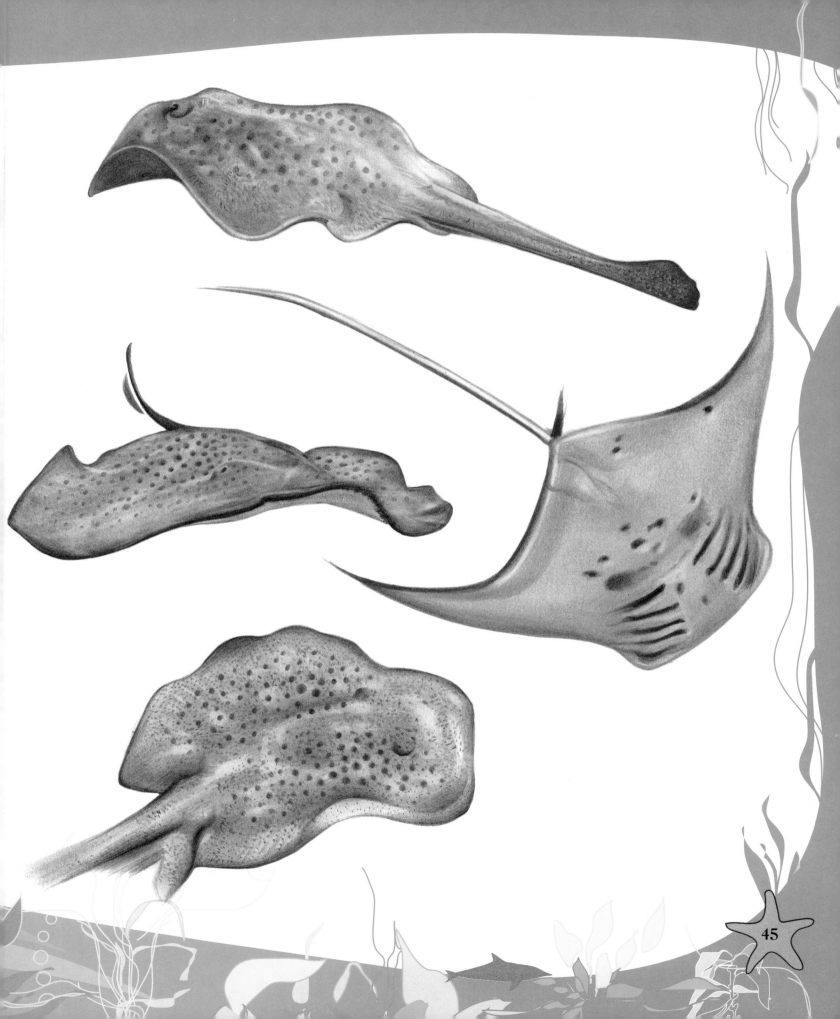

How To Draw Sharks And Their Prey

Step 1

Start by drawing a diagonal line that curves up at the top. This will be the size of the stingray's body and tail.

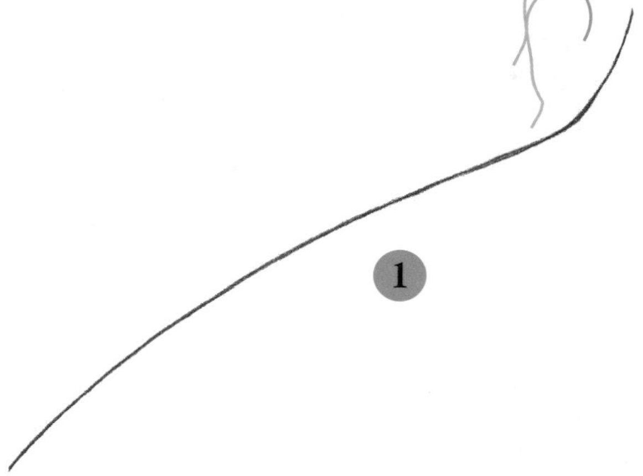

1

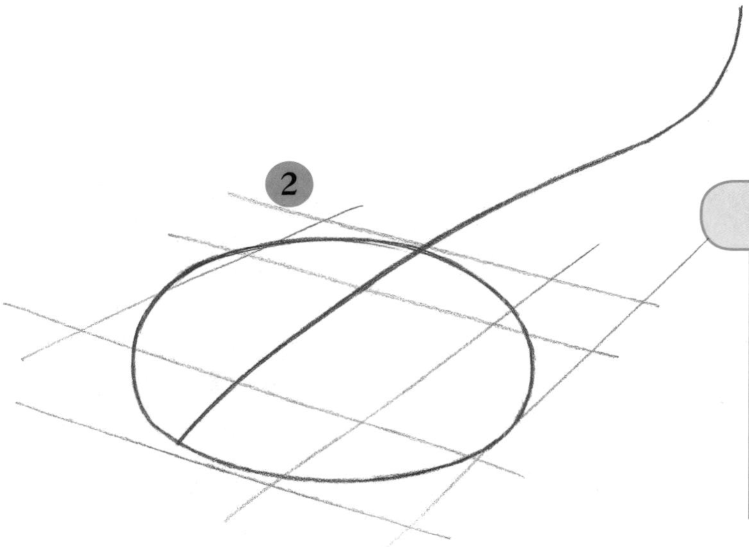

Step 2

Now draw an oval shape for the body of the ray. Lightly draw some parallel lines to help you get the perspective right.

2

Step 3

Draw two small ovals for the eyes. Determine the eye position using the diagonal line drawn earlier.

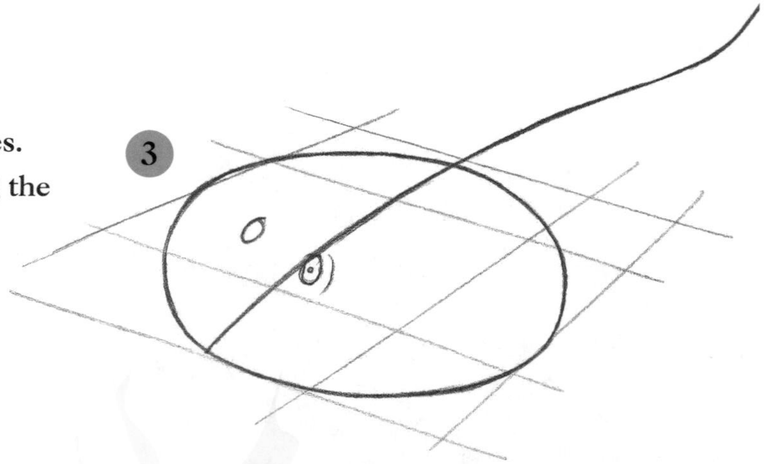

3

Step 4

Now erase the guidelines and concentrate on the contour of the ray. Draw the curved outline along the outer edge of the body, adding some details to show the thin, loose skin around the edges.

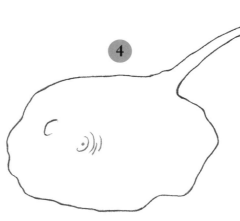

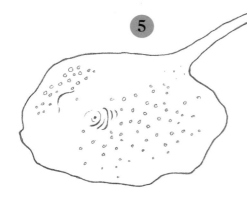

Step 5

Detail the tiny eye and add a few skin folds around it. For the spots on the body, notice that they're bigger and darker in the center, and smaller and lighter toward the edges.

Step 6

Now start with the shading. The tail will be slightly darker than the rest of the body. The body shape bulges a little in the center and is thin toward the edges. The central area gets maximum light and is lighter than the rest of the body. The skin folds around the edges are darker. You can also add a dark shadow under the folds to show raised skin.

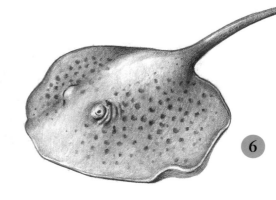

STARRY FLOUNDER

The starry flounder (*Platichthys stellatus*) lives in the coastal waters of the North Pacific Ocean. This fish can be either right-eyed or left-eyed, which means that its eyes are on the same side of its body! The eyed side is brown or black, while the blind side is white. The starry flounder can grow to be up to 3 feet (0.9 m) long and weigh around 20 pounds (9 kg). Great white and hammerhead sharks are two predators of the starry flounder.

Step 1

Start by drawing a slightly curved line to form the spine of the fish. This fish is best shown in profile and is easier to draw that way.

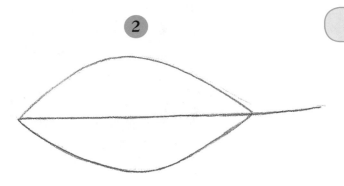

Step 2

For the basic body shape, draw an ellipse with pointed ends along the line drawn earlier. The top and lower portions should be about the same.

Step 3

Starting from the front end, draw another ellipse with a bigger bulge in the center over the top of the fish. Do the same under the fish. These will form the fins. Add a triangular shape for the tail fin. Mark the eye position quite close to the pointed end on the left side of the fish.

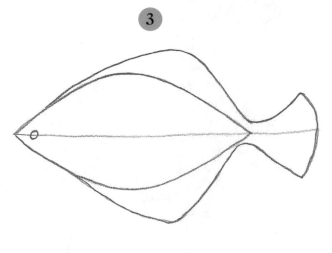

50

Step 4

Draw curved vertical lines in the top and bottom fins. Draw flat ovals on the tail. Also add a small fin in the middle of the body.

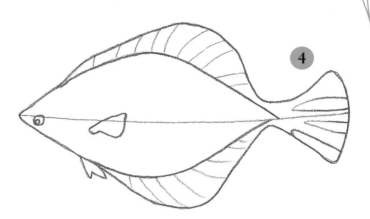

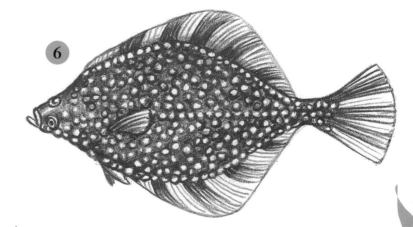

Step 5

Now add the details of the mouth and eyes. Also add the little circular scales to get the skin texture of the starry flounder.

Step 6

For the fins and tail, alternate dark and light sections. Use parallel strokes.

LOBSTER

The lobster is a cold-blooded animal that lives on the ocean floor. It has a hard skeleton on the outside of its body, three pairs of walking legs, two large front claws, and eyes that sit on top of stalks. A lobster continues to grow throughout its life and may live to be 100 years old! Lobsters are prey for many larger animals, including the hammerhead shark.

How To Draw Sharks And Their Prey

Step 1

Start with simple lines to show the parts and pose of the lobster— a tapering body, two large claws in the front, and a tail in the back.

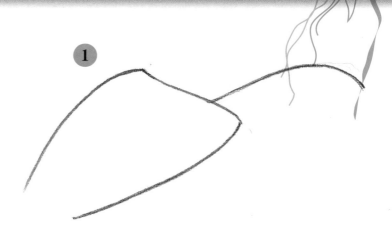

Step 2

Lightly draw the various parts of the lobster along these lines. Draw longish ovals for the jointed claws in the front; a bigger and more rounded oval for the central body; and a medium-sized oval with a sharp point for the tail. Notice the proportion of the parts to the body.

Step 3

Once you get the basic shapes and proportions in place, start adding details. Define the claws further. Draw the head portion on the body with two small ovals. Add the separations on the tail.

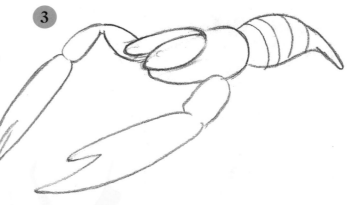

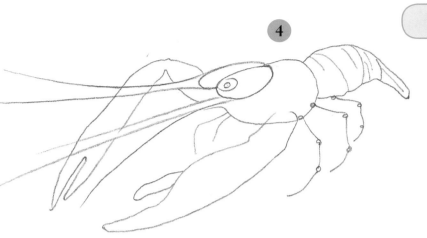

Step 4

Use your reference lines
to get the specific shapes of
the different parts of the lobster.
Lightly mark the position of
the three visible legs. Also draw
the eye and the antennae on
the head.

Step 5

Erase the light reference lines
and finalize the details.
Draw the antennae, eye,
legs, and pattern on the
lobster's body.

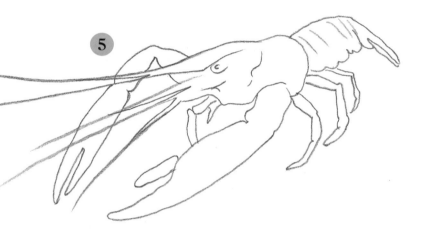

Step 6

You can now begin shading.
Start with the lighter portions, then
move to the darker ones. Take note
of the light source.

BASKING SHARK

The basking shark (*Cetorhinus maximus*) is the second largest fish in the world and is found in coastal temperate waters. It is grayish brown to black or bluish on the upper surface and off-white on its belly. It can be up to 33 feet (10 m) long and weigh up to 4 tons (3.6 metric tons). This shark is a slow swimmer with a short snout, huge gills, and bristle-like gill rakers inside its mouth that it uses to catch tiny animals (zooplankton) for food.

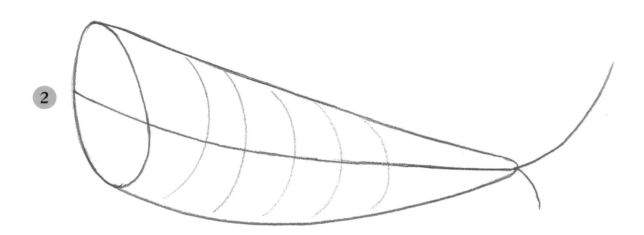

Step 1

For drawing the basking shark, start with a shallow arc as reference. This pose of the shark is below eye level.

Step 2

Draw a cone along the line with the tapering ends on the right. Lightly draw an oval at the open end of the cone. Add small arcs to the tapered end to show the tail fin. Lightly draw curved parallel lines along the cone to help you visualize a three-dimensional form.

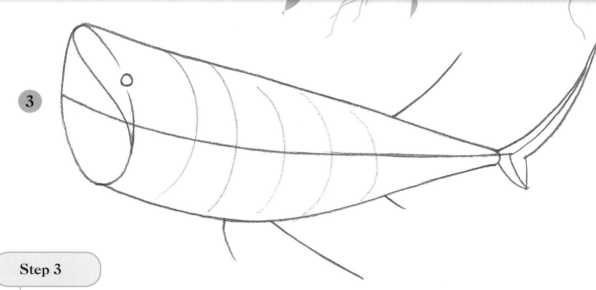

3

Now add an "S" to the oval at the open end of the cone to show the upper jaw and the gaping mouth. Also add the eye and directional lines for the fins. Add volume to the tail fin by drawing thin triangular shapes around the reference lines.

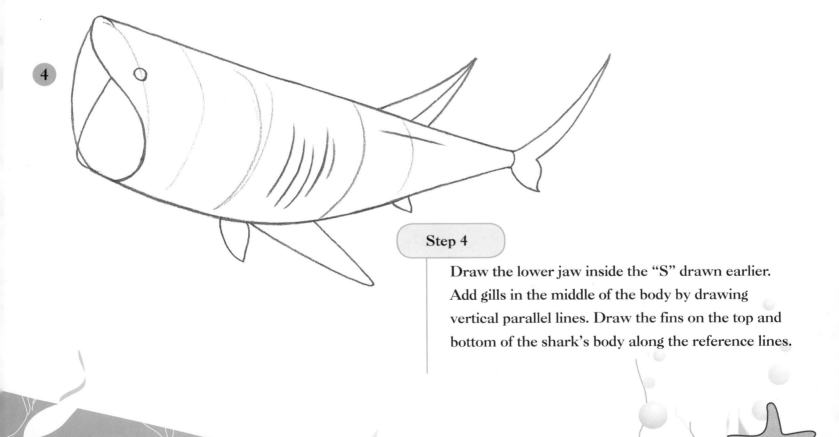

4

Step 4

Draw the lower jaw inside the "S" drawn earlier. Add gills in the middle of the body by drawing vertical parallel lines. Draw the fins on the top and bottom of the shark's body along the reference lines.

5

Step 5

Add "ribs" in a spiked pattern inside the lower jaw. The "ribs" are angular and slightly curved along the volume of the jaws.

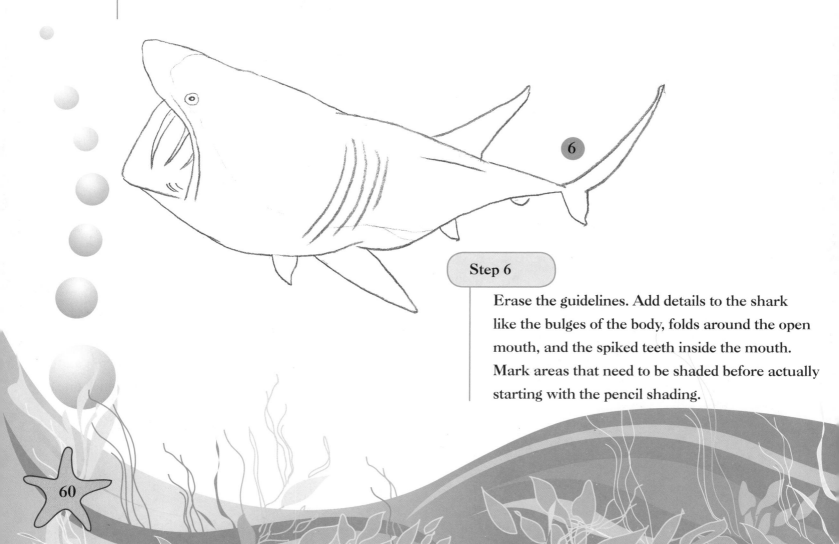

6

Step 6

Erase the guidelines. Add details to the shark like the bulges of the body, folds around the open mouth, and the spiked teeth inside the mouth. Mark areas that need to be shaded before actually starting with the pencil shading.

7

Step 7

The shaded areas are well defined for this shark—the upper part of its body is light, and the lower is darker. Notice the extra dark tones in between the gills and inside the mouth. The texture on the body is smooth, so use light, soft strokes. Use even, smooth pencil strokes for the dark areas.

Details

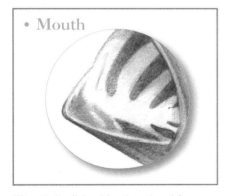

• Mouth

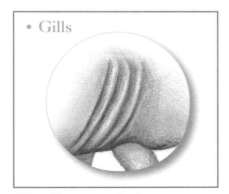

• Gills

The "ribs" inside the shark's mouth are slightly curved along the volume of the jaw. They are darker than the rest of the area, so use a 4B or 6B to render.

The gills are vertical openings on the skin in the middle of the shark's body. The lines are not exactly parallel to each other, and they follow the volume of the body in a slight curve. Shade along these lines using light to dark tones. Also add an extra dark tone (4B pencil) along the line. Make sure that the shading gradually fades out toward the end of the gill lines at the top.